LEAVING HOME
(GENESIS 11.26-32) (GENESIS 12:1-7)

Terah was the father of Abram,
Nahor, and Haran. Haran was Lot's father.
Haran died in the city of Ur.
Abram married Sarai,
but they had no children.
Terah took Abram, Lot, and Sarai
and started out for the Land of Canaan.
But they stopped and then stayed in the
City of Haran. Terah died in Haran.

*1. In this story we meet a lot of new people: Terah, Abram, Sarai, and Lot. Who are they?

2. The Torah doesn't tell us anything about Abram's mother, the mother of the first Jew— we don't even know her name. Make up one story about her.

3. What important thing is missing from Abram and Sarai's family? (*If necessary, read the story again.*) ❑ How do you think Abram and Sarai feel about not having children?

4. Abram was born in the city of Ur. The whole family left Ur. Where were they going? (*If necessary, read the text again*)

5. They never got to Canaan. Where did they stop? What happened there? ❑ Do you think they will continue their journey without Terah?

* Questions with a * are places where parents or teachers can expect to fill in extra information. These questions are asked in order to provide opportunities to teach or explain.

❑ Are follow-up questions which are to be asked after the previous questions are answered.

6. The family did not go on to Canaan on their own. Why do you think they stayed in Haran?

*7. *When God talks to Abram, God offers Abram a blessing if the family continues their journey. What is a blessing?* ❑ When God blesses Abram, what kinds of things does God promise? (*If necessary, re-read the blessings*) ❑ Which of these blessings do you think is most important? Why?

8. This question is not answered in the Torah. You'll have to decide your own reason: Why do you think God picked Abram's family to be the family who would become God's special friends?

God said to Abram:
"Take yourself
   from your land,
   from your birthplace,
   from your father's house,
to The Land: there I will let you **see**.
   And I will make you a great nation
   And I will bless you.
   And I will make your name great .
   And you will be a blessing.
   And I will bless those who bless you.
   And I will curse any one who curses you.
   All the families of the earth
     will be blessed through you."

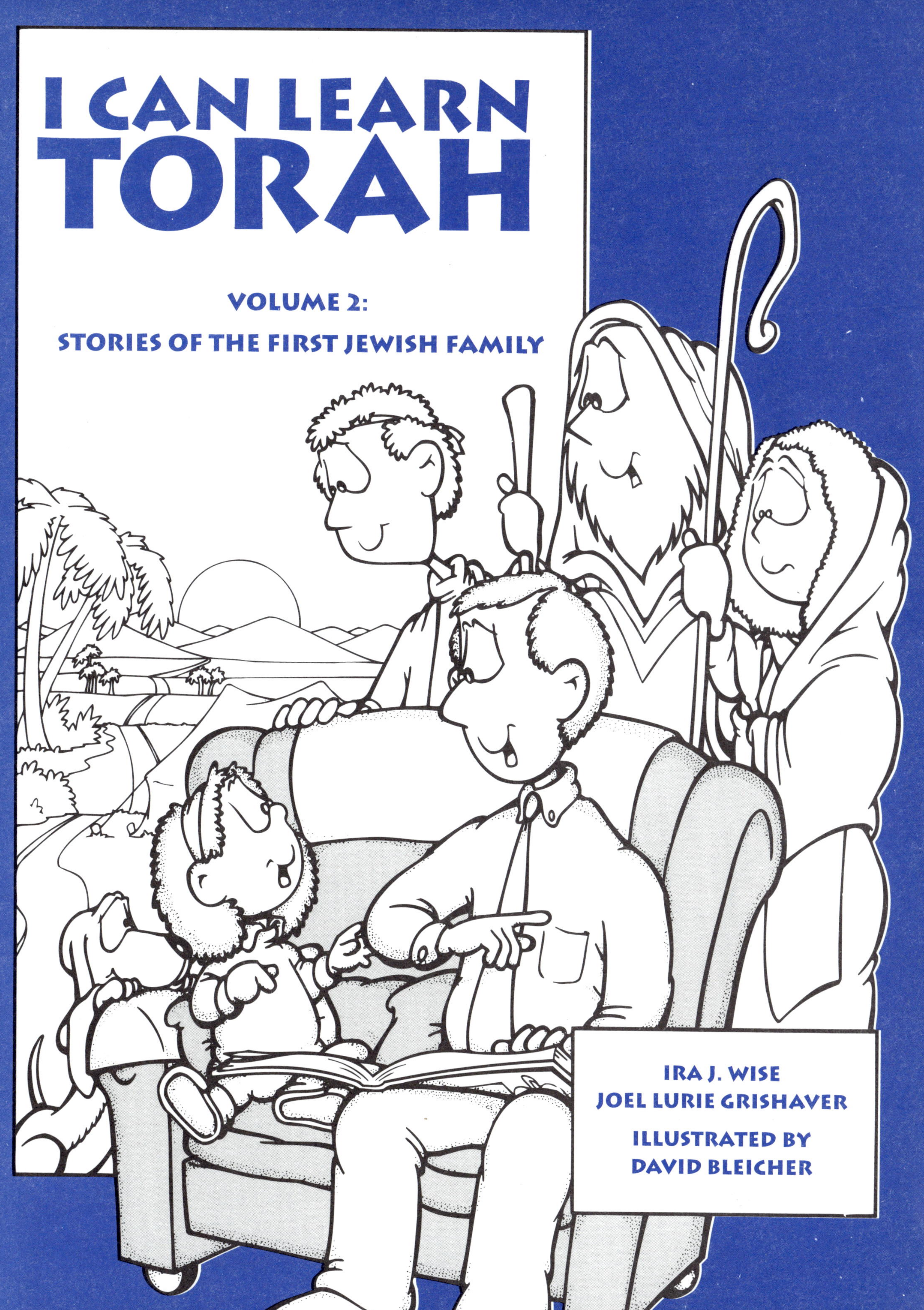

I CAN LEARN TORAH
VOLUME 2:
STORIES OF THE FIRST JEWISH FAMILY
IRA J. WISE
JOEL LURIE GRISHAVER
ILLUSTRATED BY
DAVID BLEICHER

I Can Learn Torah is a new kind of Torah study for young children. (In truth, it is a very old kind of Torah study which has been renewed—story telling). It is designed to bring Torah back as part of an "oral" tradition, and make the stories into not just parables with good morals at the end, but rather adventures which children are involved in hearing, telling, and figuring out.

I Can Learn Torah is a book which has been designed for children who are too young to effectively read and understand text on their own. It takes a parent or a teacher, or ideally a networking of home and classroom, to make this book come alive, to help the written version of the **Torah** be the beginning of the story, but not the whole story.

In writing **I Can Learn Torah** we have imagined a classroom where the story is read aloud a little bit at a time. It makes little difference whether or not the children are following along. Each page turn has been designed to create the same excitement as did the cliffhanger in old movie serials. Students are brought into the story by being asked to (1) re-state the basic facts, (2) explain how characters are feelings, and (3) guess what will happen next.

We also hope that each and every story will be reread and discussed by parents at home. We see a weekly Torah story as a great bed time event, a wonderful Shabbat table activity, or just some good quality time together. We know that students like, and need, to read stories more than once. We know that Jews discuss and learn these stories over and over, always finding something new.

We have also created a parent-teacher's guide for each volume of **I Can Learn Torah**, to help guide and enrich this process. We believe that this series is the beginning of a life long connection to Torah and to the power of all Jewish stories. We believe it creates a process which assures the future of the Jewish people. Besides, we expect it to be a lot of fun!

Ira and Joel

ISBN# 0-933873-68-9

Torah Aura Productions
4423 Fruitland Avenue
Los Angeles, California 90058
(800) BE-TORAH (213) 585-7312

MANUFACTURED IN THE UNITED STATES OF AMERICA

Abram was seventy five-years old when he left Haran.
Abram took Sarai his wife,
and Lot his nephew,
and all they owned,
and all their people,
and they left for the Land of Canaan.

10. What happens to Abram right after he arrived in Canaan? ❑ God is invisible. No one can **see** God. But, when Abram arrives in Canaan, the Torah tells us that Abram **saw** God. What do you think he **saw**?

11. God is also everywhere. Why do you think Abram **saw** God only after he came to The Land?

12. What new promise does God make to Abram after he arrives in the Land of Israel?

*13. What is an altar? What do you do with an altar? Why did Abram build one?

14. We've come to the end of the story where Sarai, Lot, and Abram move to the land of Canaan. What do you think will be the first adventure Abram, Sarai, and Lot have in the Land of Canaan?

15. *Abram, Sarai and Lot lived in ancient times, thousands of years before anyone invented a camera.* If they did have a camera, what would be three interesting pictures in their family album?

They came to the Land of Canaan.
At that time
there were still Canaanites living in The Land.
Then, God was **seen** by Abram.

God said:
"To your future-family I will give this Land."
Abram built an altar
to God Whom he had **seen**.

GOD WAS SEEN BY ABRAHAM

Draw a picture of wind.

Draw a picture of something wind does.

DISCUSSION

How is drawing a picture of God like drawing a picture of wind? If you had to draw a picture of something which God does, what would you draw?

ABRAM BUILT AN ALTAR TO GOD WHOM HE SAW

Where in each of these pictures can you find God?

____

____

____

____

THEY CAME TO THE LAND OF CANAAN...
THEN, GOD WAS SEEN BY ABRAM.

MY COMMENT:

We expect parents or teachers or teaching assistants to "take dictation" and fill in all **My Comment** exercises for the students. They are intentionally designed as *Language Experience* opportunities.

Abram felt close to God when he moved to the land which would become Israel. One time when I felt close to God is when...:

____

____

LOT LEAVES
(GENESIS 12.10) (GENESIS 13:1-15)

There was a famine in the Land of Canaan.
Abram and his family
went down to Egypt
to live there for a while
because the famine in The Land
was very bad.

*1. What is a famine?

*2. Why did Abram and his family go to Egypt? Why wasn't the famine as bad there?

3. What do people do when there is a famine today?

Later,
Abram went back up to Canaan from Egypt.
He went with his wife and **all that was his**.
Abram was very rich

    in **herds**, in **silver**, and in **gold.**
And **Lot** (who went with Abram)

    also owned

    sheep, oxen, and tents.

4. When Abram, Sarai, and Lot first came to Canaan, the Torah describes it this way (on page 5): "Abram took Sarai his wife, and Lot his nephew, and **all they owned**." What has changed since then? (*To figure out the difference you may need to read this paragraph a second time, or compare this drawing to the one on page 5.*)

5. What happened to the family? Why do you think they no longer live as if everything belongs to everyone?

6. What would it be like to live in a family where everyone shares everything? Would it be good or bad? ❏ How would it feel to have to share everything—to have nothing which was only yours? ❏ How would it be to live in a family where no one shared anything—where each thing was owned by one person? ❏ Which kind of family did Abram, Sarai, and Lot become?

7. When they got back to Canaan from Egypt, what was the big new problem they faced? ❏ Why weren't Abram and Lot's camps able to live together?

8. A feud is a fight which keeps going on. One fight leads to another. The Torah doesn't tell us what caused the herdsmen's feud. What is your guess about what started the argument? ❏

9. If you were Abram or Sarai, how would you feel about all this fighting? What would you do about it?

The land would not support
    both of them living together.
They owned so much that
    they were not able to live together.

There was feuding
    between Abram's herdsmen
    and Lot's herdsmen.

Abram then said to Lot:
"Let there be no feud
    between me and you,
    between my herdsmen
    and your herdsmen,
because we are men who are like brothers.

The whole land is before you
—please divide yourself from me.
If you go to the left, I will go to the right.
If you go to the right, I will go to the left."

10. Listening to Abram's words, how do you think he felt? ❏ Abram offers Lot the first choice of the land he wanted. God promised the land to Abram. Why do you think he offered Lot a choice?

11. Why did Abram and Lot have to separate? ❏ Was separating a good thing or a bad thing? Why?

12. What land did Lot choose? ❑ Why do you think he chose it? (If necessary, read the text again.) ❑ Was it a good choice?

13. What are the people of Sodom like? What do you think is going to happen to Lot when he tries to live near Sodom?

Lot lifted up his eyes
and saw the banks of the Jordan river.
It was a rich land with much water.
Lot chose this land, the Jordan plain.

So they were divided—
each man from his brother.
Abram lived in the land of Canaan.
Lot pitched his tents near the city of Sodom.
The people of Sodom were evil
and sinned on purpose.

THEY OWNED SO MUCH
THAT THEY WERE NOT ABLE TO LIVE TOGETHER.

Abram and Lot wanted to be **just** and do the right thing. When they separated, they wanted to be sure that each one got his own sheep. Help the herdsman divide the sheep.

Color all of אַבְרָם Abram's sheep in once color. They have an א ALEF branded upon them.

Color all of לוֹט's sheep another color. They have a ל LAMED branded upon them.

LET THERE BE NO FEUD BETWEEN ME AND YOU... BECAUSE WE ARE MEN WHO ARE LIKE BROTHERS.

שָׁלוֹם בַּיִת

Shalom Bayit means "Family Peace". Abram and Lot thought that *Shalom Bayit* was very important. Even though they wanted to stay together, they separated for the sake of making *shalom*.

How would you make *Shalom Bayit* in each of these cases?

3 kids and 2 candy bars

4 family members want to watch different programs

2 friends who each think they are the best at basketball.

2 kids; each wants to light the Hanukkah candle on the first night

MY COMMENT:

When Abram decided that it was best that he and Lot separate, it was a hard decision. He decided that **Shalom Bayit** was the most important thing. One thing I once had to do for the sake of **Shalom Bayit** was:

____

____

COVENANTS (GENESIS 13:14-15, 15:5-7, 17:1-27)

God said to Abram
after Lot was divided from him:
"Lift up your eyes and look around.
      North, South, East, and West.
All the land which you see,
I give it to you
and to your future-family
forever.

"Your future-family will be
like the dust covering the land.
Like the dust of the land,
your future-family
will be impossible to count."

1. *In this story God gives Abram and Sarai's family two promises:* What does God promise about the land of Canaan? What does God promise about the family's future?

2. When you stand on a mountain, and look out at everything you can see, how do you feel? ❑ If someone promised you that you were going to own everything you could see from your mountain, how would you feel?

3. Sarai and Abram have no children. In this story God promises Abram that his future-family will be huge but Abram and Sarai are old. It is too late from them to have children. Do you think this second promise will come true? ❑ Do you think Abram and Sarai believed this second promise?

Another night
God took Abram outside and said:
"Look at the sky.
Count the stars, if you can count them.
This is the number of your future-family.

"I will give this land to your future-family."

Abram trusted God. He had faith.
God felt good about Abram's trust.

4. When you go out on a dark night and look at all of the stars in the sky, how do you feel? ❏ How do you think Abram felt that night?

*5. On this page God repeats the same two promises. What are the two things God promises? ❏ What will make it difficult for each one to come true?

When Abram was 99 years old
God appeared to Abram and said:
   "I am God,
   walk before me
   and be the best.
I put My covenant between Me and you.

"I will make you very, very many.
You will become the father of many nations.
No longer will your name be **Abram**.
Instead your name will be **Abraham**
I will make you into **Abraham**
because **Abraham** means:
'The father of many nations.'
This is an everlasting covenant.
I will be God to you and to your future-family.

"I will give to you and to your future-family,
The land where you are staying.
All the land of Canaan will be yours forever."

*6. How are the promises God makes to Abram on this page the same as ones God has made before? What is different about these promises?

*7. What is the name of the deal which Abram makes with God?
❏ What is a covenant?

8. What is the new name that God gives Abram? What does it mean?

9. *Abraham is 99 years old. That is very old to become a father for the first time. It must have been hard for him and Sarai to believe that they would be parents of a new nation. Do you think that becoming* **Abraham** *helped him believe in God's promises?*

10. We think that the name **Sarai** means "princess." We don't know exactly what **Sarah** means. *The Torah doesn't explain the new name the way it explains that* **Abraham** *means "Father of a Great Nation."* It keeps the meaning of **Sarah** a secret. Take your best guess about the secret promise hidden in the name **Sarah**.

God said to Abraham:
"As for **Sarai** your wife
—don't call her **Sarai** anymore,
because **Sarah** is now her name.
I will bless her
and I will give you a son from her.
I will bless her
and nations and rulers will come from her."

COUNT THE STARS

God makes two promises to Abram. In the **first** promise God tells Abram that his future-family will have as may people as there are stars in the sky.

Count the stars in this picture.

How many stars did you find? _________
If you go out on a dark night and count the stars in the sky, how many will you find?

God makes a second promise, too. In the **second** promise, God promises to give a special land to Abram's **future-family**. It will be a place they can call home. Once this land was called Canaan. When you color in this map you'll learn its new name.

Use these Colors:
1-BLUE 2-GREEN 3-BROWN
4-RED 5-YELLOW

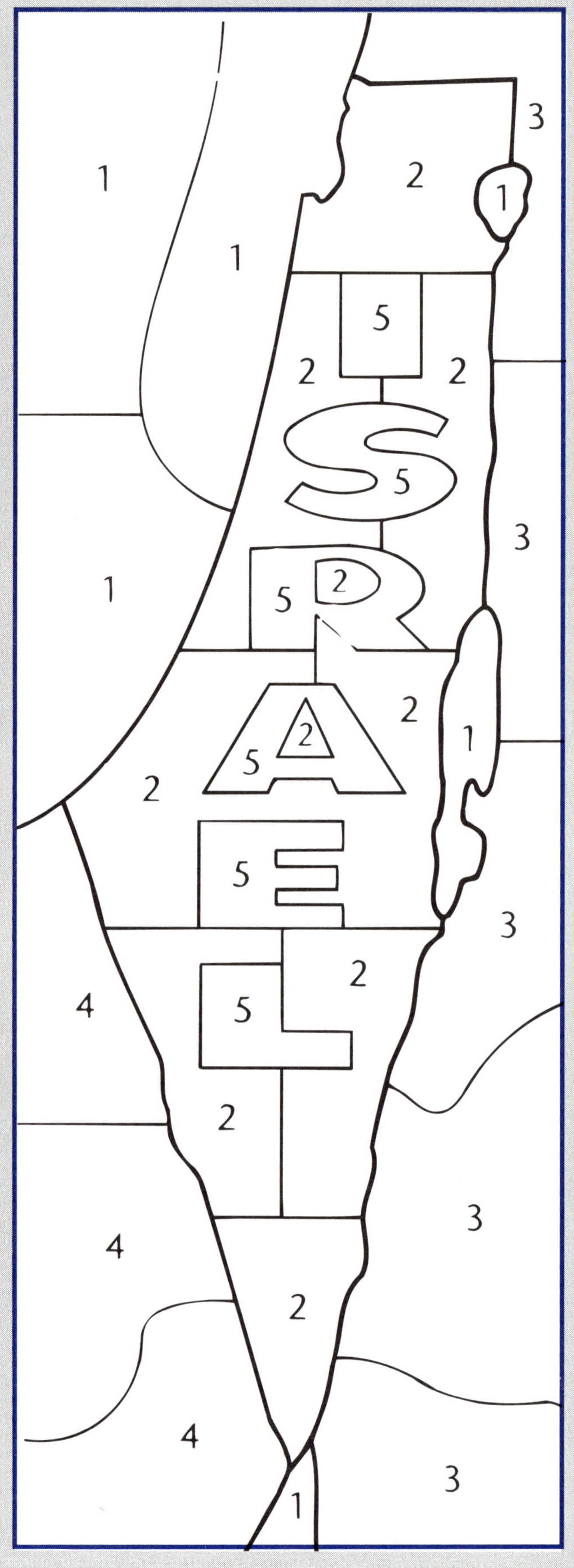

God made two promises to Abraham about his family's future. If I could ask God to make two promises to me about my family's future, they would be:

1. ____

2. ____

SARAH LAUGHED
(GENESIS 18:1-16)

God appeared to Abraham.
Abraham was camped
under the trees of Mamre,
sitting in the doorway of his tent
during the heat of the day.

*1. If you looked at Abraham and Sarah's camp from the top of a nearby hill what would you see? ❑ What do you think that Abraham could see from his tent?

2. *We have talked about this before. God is invisible, yet the Torah tells us that Abraham saw God.* The Torah begins this story by telling us that God **appeared** to Abraham—what do you think Abraham saw this time?

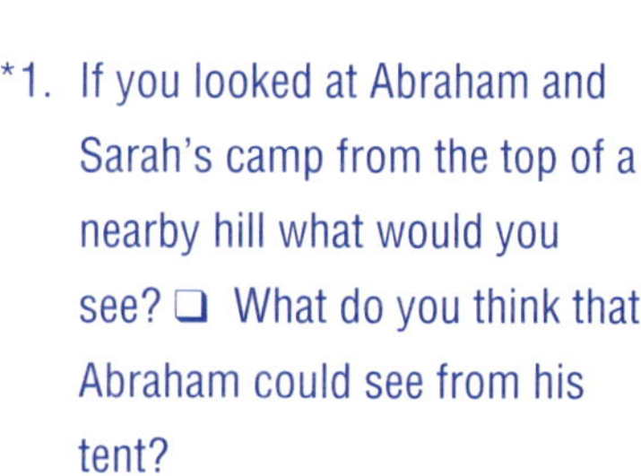

3. Abraham looked out from his tent a second time and saw something different. What did he see?

4. As soon as he saw the men, Abraham ran towards them. Why do you think he ran?

Abraham looked again and saw.
Suddenly,
three men were standing before him.
He looked once more,
and saw, and then ran to greet them.

He said: "My lords,
please, if I have found favor in your eyes,
please do not pass by me.
Please let a little water be brought to you.
So that you can wash your feet
and rest under the tree.
Let me bring you some bread."

They said: "Do just what you have said."

*5. When Abraham talks to the men, what does he offer to do? ❑ Abraham offers the men water, but where will he get it? He offers the men bread, but where will it come from?

6. Abraham says "**Please**" all the time and almost begs the visitors to let him take care of them. He acts as if the visitors are doing him a favor. What does Abraham want from the visitors? Why do you think Abraham is being so nice?

Abraham **hurried** into Sarah's tent. He said: "**Hurry**! Take three measures of good flour—knead it and bake bread."

Abraham **ran** to the herd.
He took a tender calf
and gave it to a servant,
so that he could **hurry** to prepare it.
He took yogurt and milk
and the calf which had been cooked,
and served it to them.
He stood by them under the tree
while they ate.

They said to him:
"Where is Sarah, your wife?"
And he said: "Right here in the tent."
One said:
"Sarah your wife will have a son."
Sarah was listening
at the entrance to the tent.
Abraham and Sarah were old.
Sarah was too old to have a child.
Sarah laughed inside and said to herself:
"Now that my time for having children has
passed, how can my old husband and I
have a child?"

9. What happens after dinner? ❏ What is promised to Abraham and Sarah? ❏ Why is this an important promise?

10. What does Sarah do when she hears this promise? Do you think she believes the promise?

*11. People laugh for many different reasons. What are some the reasons people laugh? ❏ *In this story, Sarah who is very old, laughs when the visitors promise her a son.* Why was she laughing? What kind of laugh was it? *Do you think Sarah was laughing at a joke, laughing to keep from crying, or doing a different kind of laughing*?

12. What does God ask Abraham?
❑ If God knows everything, God doesn't need to ask questions. Why do you think God asks Abraham about Sarah's laugh?
13. God then asks Abraham, "Is any miracle too great for God?" What is your answer to that question?
14. *The Torah tells us that Sarah was afraid. It does not tell us of what she was afraid.* Why do you think Sarah was scared? How do you think God felt about Sarah and her laugh?

God said to Abraham:
"Why is Sarah laughing and saying:
'Will I really give birth,
now that I am so old?'
Is any miracle too great for God?"
Sarah denied it.
She said: "I did not laugh."
She was afraid.
God said: "You did so laugh."

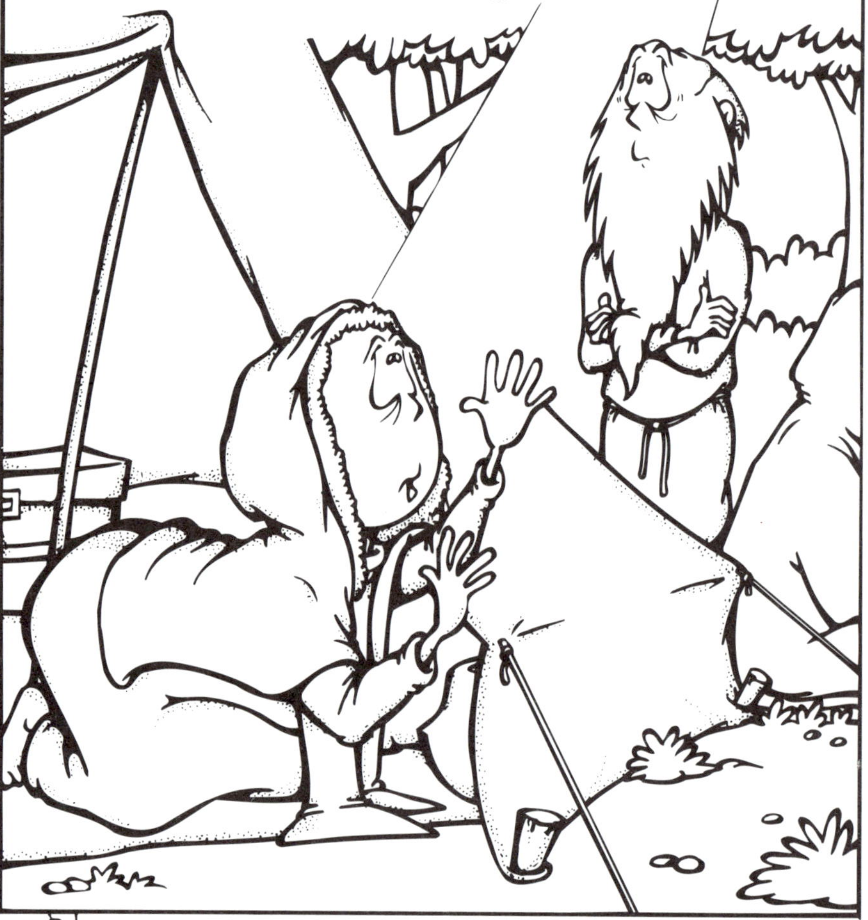

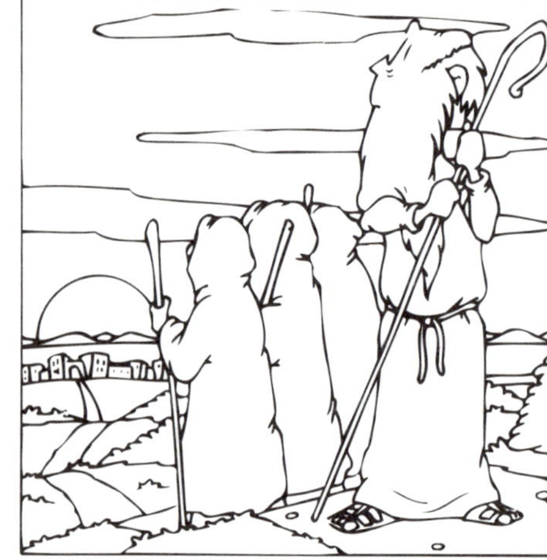

And the men got up from there and went toward Sodom. Abraham walked with them for a while. Then he sent them on their way.

14. Why do you think Abraham walked with the visitors?

HE LOOKED ONCE MORE, AND SAW, AND THEN RAN TO GREET THEM.

Help Abraham do the *mitzvah* of *Hakhnasat Orakhim*, welcoming visitors. Abraham needs the following things: *Pitcher of water, bread, calf, plate, fork, knife, spoon.* Hurry and help him find them.

SARAH LAUGHED INSIDE AND SAID TO HERSELF...

The Torah teaches us that Sarah was the first Jewish woman. Jewish women do many things. Which of these things do Jewish women do today? Which of them do Jewish men do?

Put an **W** next to everything a Jewish woman can do.

Put an **M** next to everything a Jewish man can do.

1. Become a rabbi

2. Give Birth

3. Light Shabbat candles

4. Collect money for tzedakah

5. Read from the Torah

6. Wear a tallit

7. Bake hallah

8. Teach Torah to their Children

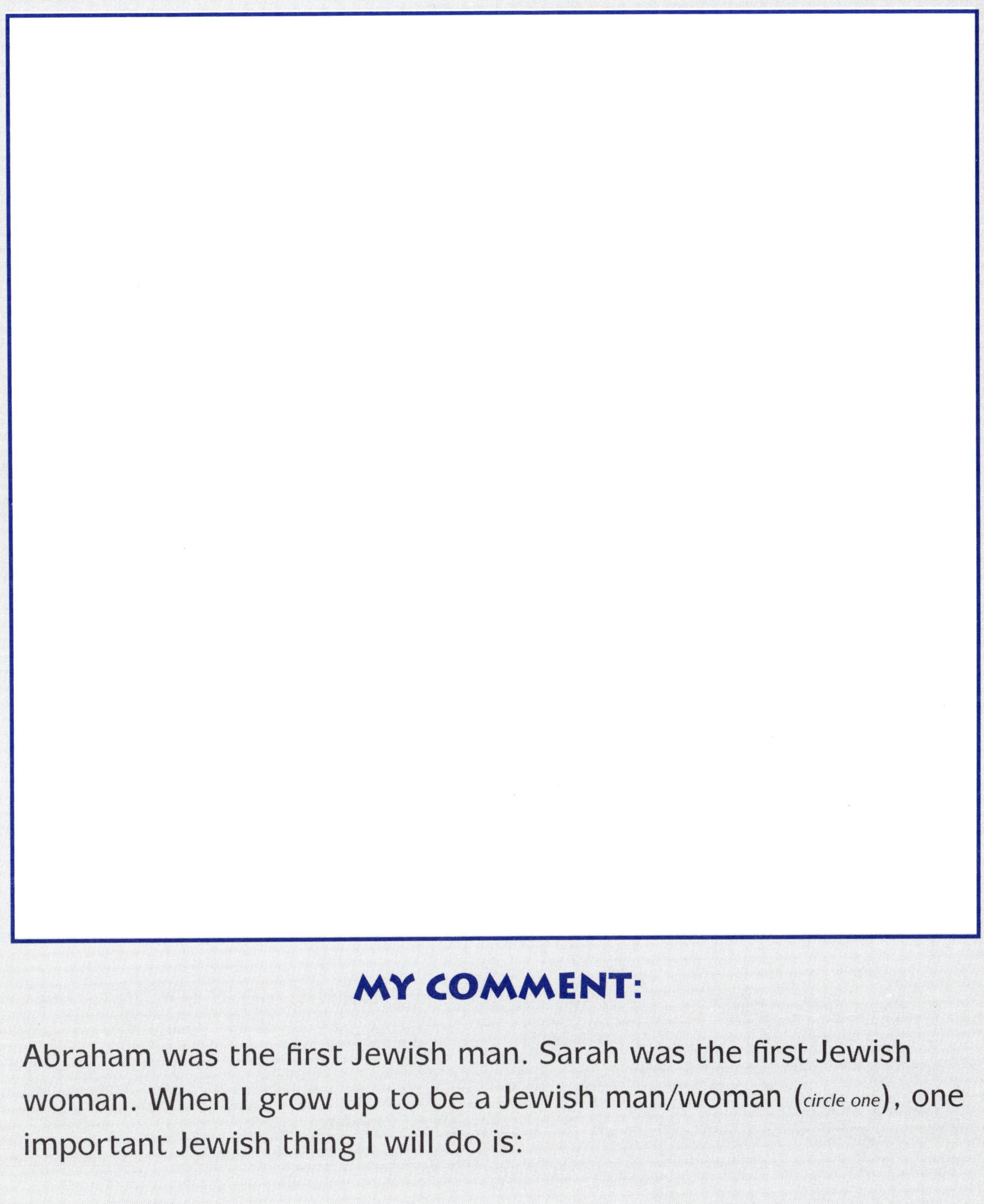

MY COMMENT:

Abraham was the first Jewish man. Sarah was the first Jewish woman. When I grow up to be a Jewish man/woman (*circle one*), one important Jewish thing I will do is:

____

____

1. *In this story we learn that God is going to destroy Sodom and Gomorah.* Why? ❏ *The Torah says, "**Their sin is very heavy**." *(You may need to define "sin.")* If you went to the cities of Sodom and Gomorah, what kinds of sins would you see the people doing?

2. In this story we learn that God has a plan for Abraham and Sarah's family. What is that plan?

3. We also learn that God must make a decision. What must God decide? (*A re-reading may be necessary*) ❏ The Torah tells us why God might want to tell Abraham about Sodom and Gomorah's future. Why would God want to tell him about it? ❏ The Torah doesn't tell us why God might not want to tell Abraham? Why might God want to keep it secret?

4. What do you think God will decide? Will God tell Abraham?

(*Optional*) 5. God says that the Jews will do what is **right** and **just** and keep God's ways. What does it mean to keep God's ways? What kinds of things does a keeper do?

God said:
"The shouting
from Sodom and Gomorah
is very loud.
Their sin is very heavy.
I am going to destroy them.
But, can I hide what I am going to do
from Abraham?
After all Abraham
is going to become a great and numerous
nation.
I have become especially close to him
so that he will command
　his children
　and his future-family
to keep God's way
and to do what is **right** and **just**."

God decided to tell Abraham.

Abraham came close to God and said:
"Will You really sweep away
the righteous people with the guilty ones?
Maybe there are 50 **righteous** people
in the city—
Will You still sweep it away?
Won't You put up with the city
if there are 50 **righteous** people there?
You above all should not do this thing,
killing the **righteous** with the wicked,
as if there were no difference
between the **righteous** and the wicked.

Should not the **Judge**-Of-All-The-Earth
do what is **just**?"

6. When God tells Abraham of the plans for Sodom and Gomorah, what does Abraham do? ❑ How does Abraham try to convince God to change the plan?

7. *Usually we think that everything God does is right. That's one of the things which makes God, God. Here, Abraham is very brave. He tells God that God's plan is wrong. Did Abraham do the right thing?* ❑ How do you think Abraham felt when he argued with God?

8. *Many Jews who have studied this story have thought that God is testing Abraham. What is the test? Do you think that Abraham passed?*

9. *Abraham changed God's mind. Originally, God was going to destroy Sodom no matter what. Abraham convinced God to save the city if there were 50 good people in it. The Torah doesn't tell us what God was thinking. Why do you think God changed the plan?*

10. *What do you think Abraham will do next?*

11. *After God agreed not to destroy the cities if 50 righteous people could be found, what does Abraham do? ❏ This happens over and over. Do you think Abraham had a plan? Or do you think each time he won, Abraham then decided to ask for more? ❏ Abraham stops at ten. He doesn't ask for five or for one. Why do you think Abraham stopped?*

12. After the conversation God leaves. Where did God go? How do you think God felt about Abraham after this conversation?

13. If it was your job to go into the cities of Sodom and Gomorah and find ten righteous people, what would you do? What would you look for? ❏ Do you think you would be able to find ten righteous people?

14. What do you think will happen to Sodom and Gomorah?

THE SHOUTING FROM SODOM AND GOMORAH IS VERY LOUD. THEIR SIN IS VERY HEAVY.

Here is a picture of a street in Sodom. Circle the people who are doing righteous things.

In the next story, God sends messengers into the city of Sodom to look for righteous people. Hidden on this page is the name of the one righteous family they find. Can you find it?

S	R	M	T	M	Z	W	Q	V	K
D	Y	N	R	Q	Y	Q	Z	T	L
F	P	L	O	T	B	P	W	G	P
G	M	Y	B	R	M	Y	S	B	M
H	N	T	L	S	C	T	X	Y	J
J	B	R	Q	J	N	G	D	H	N
K	Q	J	R	B	V	H	C	N	H
T	X	H	S	M	K	F	R	J	Z
R	F	C	T	D	S	J	F	C	B
W	W	M	P	X	D	G	R	M	V

MY COMMENT

In this story Abraham asks God to change God's plans. If I could ask God to change one thing about the world, I would ask God to:

____

____

TWO MORE STORIES

The Torah is a very long book. It takes a whole lifetime to learn it. We are not going to discuss two important stories, but we think you should know about them.

THE DESTRUCTION OF SODOM (GENESIS 19.1-30)

The story of Sodom continues. Two of God's messengers come to the city of Sodom. They meet Lot at the city gate. Like Abraham, he invites them home as guests. That night the people of the town gather to hurt the two strangers, but Lot protects his guests. Before dawn, Lot's family sneaks out of the city with the messengers. The messengers warn the family not to look back.

God destroys Sodom and Gomorah. Lot's wife turns to look back and becomes a pillar of salt. Abraham watches the destruction from far away. Lot and his daughters move to a cave in the hills.

HAGAR AND ISHMAEL (16.1-14, 21.9-21)

When Sarah was still Sarai she felt bad that Abraham (who was still Abram) did not have a son. She did something we would not do today. She had an Egyptian slave woman named Hagar. (We no longer have slaves). She told Abram to take Hagar as his second-class wife. (Today, Jewish men only have one wife *at a time*—no matter what.) Hagar and Abraham had a son named "Ishmael."

Sarah and Hagar didn't get along. There was also some kind of problem between Ishmael and Isaac. (Isaac is the son who will be born to Abraham and Sarah in the next chapter). Eventually, to keep *shalom bayit*, Abraham sends Ishmael and Hagar away. Ishmael too, becomes the father of a great nation: the Arab peoples. After all, he, too, was Abraham's son.

ISAAC IS BORN
(GENESIS 21:1-8)

God remembered Sarah
just as God had promised.
Sarah became pregnant
and gave birth to a son.
Abraham named his son Isaac
(meaning "He Laughs").
Abraham circumcised his son.
Abraham was 100 years old
when Isaac was born.
Sarah said: "God has made laughter for me.
Everyone who hears will laugh with me."
The boy grew
and Abraham gave a party on the day
that Isaac began eating solid food.

2. What does "Isaac" mean? ❏ What other story do you remember when Sarah laughs?

*3. What did Isaac eat before he could eat solid food? ❏ What made "weaning" from breast feeding a good time for a party?

4. What do you think happened at Isaac's party? What was it like?

ABRAHAM NAMED HIS SON ISAAC

Draw a picture of each of these people being their names:

Eve	Noah	Abraham	Isaac
Giver of Life	God is Comfortable	Father of a Great Nation	Laughter

This story tells us that God _________________ Sarah. Fill in the missing letter in each of these names, and read down to find the answer.

SA_AH

AB_L

SODO_

_VE

ADA_

BA_EL

_GYPT

AB_AHAM

ISRA_L

E_EN

God _________________ Sarah by giving her a child. One way I would like God to _______________ me, is:

____

SARAH DIES AND ABRAHAM BUYS A CAVE
(GENESIS 23.1-19)

Sarah lived one-hundred and twenty seven years. She died in the land of Canaan. Abraham mourned Sarah and cried for her.

1. *Sarah lived a good and long life, 127 years.* How do you think Abraham felt when she died? ❏ **The Torah tells us that Abraham mourned for Sarah.* What does it mean to mourn?

2. Abraham cried for a long time. Why do you think he stopped?

3. *When someone dies, Jews gather together and sit shiva. It is a week of mourning and comforting. One of the things which people do during shiva is remember things about the person who has died. Sarah has just died.* What do you remember about her?

Abraham went
to speak to the Families-of-<u>H</u>et.
He said "I am a stranger
who is living among you.
Let me own a burying-place among you
that I may bury my dead."
The Families-of-<u>H</u>et answered Abraham:
"Listen, you are God's chosen
living among us.
In the best of our burying-places,
bury your dead.
No one of us will hold back
his burial-place from you."

4. Why does Abraham go to the Families-of-<u>H</u>et?

5. Abraham says to the Families-of-<u>H</u>et: "I am a stranger who is living among you." Abraham has been living in the land of Canaan for more than sixty years. Why do you think he calls himself a stranger? ❏ What is it like to be a stranger?

6. *Abraham wants to use the cave of the Makhpelah as his family burial place.* How does he want to take ownership of it? ❏ *Ephron, one of the People-of-Het, owned the field and the cave. He is willing to let Abraham use his cave.* How does he want Abraham to use it?

7. What do you think Abraham should do about Ephron's offer? Why?

Abraham bowed
before the people of the land,
and said to Ephron
so that everyone could hear:
"I will buy the field with silver.
Take the silver from me
and I will bury my dead there."
And Ephron answered Abraham,
"Four hundred shekels of silver
what is that between you and me?
Give it to me and then bury your dead."
Abraham then paid Ephron
After this, Abraham buried Sarah, his wife,
in the cave of the Makhpelah
And Abraham took ownership
of the field and the cave
as an ever-owned burying-place
among the Families-of-<u>H</u>et.

8. What deal do Abraham and Ephron make? ❏ Do you think it was a good deal?

9. *Buying the Cave of the Makhpelah was very important to Abraham. He refused to accept it as a gift. Instead, he makes sure that everyone in the town knew about the deal he made to buy the cave.* Why do you think it was important to Abraham to buy the cave (and not accept it as a gift)?

10. Abraham is an old man. His wife is dead. His sons have grown up. He is rich and has a big camp. What interesting adventures do you think he will have next?

GOD REMEMBERED SARAH

Put these Sarah events in order:

Sarah gives birth to Isaac

God gives Sarai a new name

Sarah laughs

Sarah Says Goodbye to Lot

Abraham tells Sarah about the Covenant

Sarah leaves <u>H</u>aran and comes to Canaan

Sarah cooks for three visitors

Sarah has a party when Isaac can eat solid food

MY COMMENT

Abraham spent sixty years as a
stranger in the land of Israel. In this
story, he took the first steps toward
making Israel the home of the Jewish
people. When I go to the Land of
Israel, the first place I want to see is

**And these words that I make MITZVOT for you today
shall be on your HEART.
You should TEACH them to your children
and you should TALK about them
when you SIT at home and when you GO out
when you LIE down and when you get UP.**

Deuteronomy 6:6-7

Pupils who spent 10 minutes of leisure time every day reading a book not only were star performers in classroom reading but had made steady gains in reading achievement between second and fifth grade.

Time spent at the dinner table also improves reading. Table talk may promote discussions which can stimulate interests, support and extend new learnings and broaden children's frame of reference.

Time spent doing chores was also associated with greater reading proficiency.

Reading Research Quarterly, Volume 23, No. 3, Page 285

Q: When should parents begin to teach children Torah?

A: A ... **s
should** ... **ses
made t** ... **y
33:4) a** ... **6:4)
As they** ... **teach them
more and more.**

Moses Maimonides, Mishneh Torah, Laws of Torah Study, 1.6

**TORAH AURA PRODUCTIONS, 4423 FRUITLAND AVENUE, LOS ANGELES, CA 90058
(800) BE-TORAH   (213) 585-7312**